Praise for *God's Mighty Men*

God's Mighty Men is a book written for men wanting to learn what it means to live for God. Carlos Marshall offers tried and proven methodology to be better at love, leadership, and life. This book should be required reading for men's Bible study and small groups across the nation.
— Pastor James T. Murkison, Voices of Faith South

"Pastor Carlos Marshall is a prime example of how to handle challenges with God's grace. I am thankful for access to his wisdom and knowledge. My prayer is that *God's Mighty Men* encourages, enhances, and enlightens men regardless of beliefs."
— Pastor Vincent E. Harris; House of Bethel Christian Church

God gave Carlos answers to secrets for which men have spent years searching. *God's Mighty Men* is an empowering book with fresh perspective, firsthand insight, and proven results.
— Pastor B. Buckley, Voices of Faith Church Baton Rouge

Pastor Carlos is always willing to serve, pray, or teach. The character of this mighty man of God shines through everything he does. *God's Mighty Men* will enlighten you to let God be dominant in every area of your life.

—Mother Eva Woodside

"*God's Mighty Men* communicates the difficult aspects of relationships from a man's perspective and is informative on how to improve relationships in a godly way.

—Pastor Francisco Clark, Devine Love Church

God's Mighty Men

The Christian Man's Guide to Love, Leadership, and Life

By

Carlos K. Marshall

Published by
Queen V Publishing
Englewood, OH
QueenVPublishing.com

Published by
Queen V Publishing
Englewood, OH
QueenVPublishing.com

Library of Congress Catalog Number: 2021908212

ISBN-13: 978-0-9962991-7-6

Edited by Valerie J. Lewis Coleman of Pen of the Writer PenOfTheWriter.com

Printed in the United States of America

Dedication

I dedicate this book to my children — Camen, Maya, and Cayla — as part of my legacy to you. You fill my heart with love and push me to be the best father.

The proverbs of Solomon the son of
David, king of Israel:
To know wisdom and instruction, to
perceive the words of understanding,
to receive the instruction of wisdom,
justice, judgment, and equity;
— Proverbs 1:1-3

Acknowledgments

Thank you to everyone who walked with me on the journey to complete *God's Mighty Men*:

My children: Camen, Maya, and Cayla

My mother, Deloris Marshall

My sister, Tara Nunley

My mentor, Jimmy Smith

My pastor and spiritual father, Bishop Gary Hawkins

My Voices of Faith East church family

My close friends and proofreaders: Deena Wingard and Sharahanne Gibbons

My publisher, writing coach, and mentor, Valerie J. Lewis Coleman

My son, if you receive my words, and treasure my commands within you, so that you incline your ear to wisdom, and apply your heart to understanding; yes, if you cry out for discernment, and lift up your voice for understanding,
—Proverbs 2:1-3

Table of Contents

My son, do not forget my law, but let
your heart keep my commands; for
length of days, long life and peace they
will add to you.
Let not mercy and truth forsake you;
bind them around your neck, write
them on the tablet of your heart,
— Proverbs 3:1-3

Foreword

"Falling in love is easy. Staying in love—that's the challenge. How can you keep your relationship fresh and growing amid the demands, conflicts, and just plain boredom of everyday life?"
—Dr. Gary Chapman, author of *The Five Love Languages*

Relationships can be challenging. Because the man and woman grew up in different environments with varying cultures, religious beliefs, core values and life experiences, merging lives can be cumbersome and difficult. Despite the vast differences, the couple is expected to become one in marriage. This oneness does not happen without challenges.

The top relationship challenge is ineffective communication. Often, blame is placed on the man for not articulating his feelings, thoughts and concerns. Men have a reputation for shutting down, walking away from a heated discussion, and in some cases, avoiding conversations resulting in the myth that men are not effective communicators. I believed this myth until I started counseling married couples over 25 years ago.

I assumed women were better communicators, until I realized that women are better at expressing themselves, which does not necessarily equate to good communication. A good communicator listens well and then responds accordingly. Many men are not gifted with — nor nurtured for — self-expression; however, they often listen more than they speak.

God's Mighty Men written by my spiritual son, Pastor Carlos Marshall, is a must-read masterpiece that was long overdue! He destroys the myth that men are not effective communicators by drawing upon his personal example as a nurturing, loving man. *God's Mighty Men* takes you on a journey that will forever change your perspective. Marriages and relationships will be saved, restored and strengthened as the gap between the sexes narrows. For many years, I witnessed how Pastor Marshall treats his wife and children; which qualifies him to write such an amazing book. My prayer is that you read with an open mind and discover that *God's Mighty Men* express emotions, show sensitivity, and communicate effectively.

Bishop Gary Hawkins, Sr.
Founder and senior pastor of Voices of Faith Ministries
VoicesFaith.org

Does not wisdom cry out, and
understanding lift up her voice?
She takes her stand on the top of the
high hill, beside the way,
where the paths meet.
— Proverbs 8:1-2

Introduction

If you are like me, you have been accused of:

- Poor communication
- Being unable – or unwilling – to deal with emotional situations
- Commitment phobia
- Inadequate nurturing
- Not paying attention to detail
- Being unapologetic in word or deed
- Being unable to multi-task
- Being driven by sex without concern for romance

God placed in my spirit that not all men are what society says, so I wrote this book to encourage Christian men to never give up on their marriage. *God's Mighty Men* is not an exclusive club or elitist group that only certain men can join. The men who lift up a standard for others to emulate did not choose the mantle. God chose them.

Despite his shortcomings, King David was a man after God's own heart. He loved God's people, sought Him for counsel, and obeyed His instruction...most of the time. He surrounded himself with mighty men who supported him, protected him, and accompanied him to defeat the Philistine giants on numerous occasions (2 Samuel 2:8-39). He trusted them with his life and they respected his authority and leadership.

Like David's Mighty Men, God expects us to love, lead and live for Him. Can He trust you to be one of *God's Mighty Men*?

To reinforce the message, I provided reflections at the end of each chapter. Spend time assessing yourself and your marriage to generate a more fruitful union.

Pastor Carlos K. Marshall
Pastor of Voices of Faith East
CarlosKMarshall.com

Chapter 1

God's Men Communicate

Have you ever played the Whisper Game? Teams line up with members standing one behind the other. A message is given to the first person of each team, who must remember, and then whisper it to the person behind them. This chain of communication continues through the team. When the last person receives the message, they repeat what they heard. With 100% assuredness, the final message is distorted beyond recognition of the original. When the starting message is stated aloud, everyone erupts into laughter at the confusion and chaos created by misunderstanding. The fast-paced, fun activity is great for a game. Not so much for your relationship.

Per an online article by Smriti Chand[1], communication is an exchange of facts or ideas to achieve mutual harmony. The process of establishing common ground consists of seven major elements:

1. Sender/Communicator: The person who conveys the message with the intention of passing information and ideas to others.

2. Ideas: The subject matter of the communication consisting of opinions, attitudes, feelings, views, orders, or suggestions.

3. Encoding: Since the idea is intangible, communicating it requires use of symbols like words, actions, or pictures. Converting ideas into these symbols is encoding.

4. Communication Channel: The method used to transmit information to the receiver can be

---

[1] *7 Major Elements of the Communication Process,* YourArticleLibrary.com online: http://www.yourarticlelibrary.com/business-communication/7-major-elements-of-communication-process/25815 (accessed March 27, 2020).

formal or informal. Examples include face-to-face, phone, email, text, or letter.

5. Receiver: The person who receives the message or for whom the message is intended.

6. Decoding: The receiver attempts to decipher the sender's message by converting the symbols and extracting their meaning to gain understanding.

7. Feedback: The process of ensuring the receiver received and understood the message as the sender intended.

As you can see, it's easy for a message to be misunderstood, distorted, or lost. Considering other variables like differences in how men and women communicate, nonverbal communication, and love languages, it's no wonder mastering effective communication is a full-time commitment.

To be effective at communication, I express my feelings and share what is going on in my life. Initiating dialogue breaks the ice when a person does not want to share. Detailed communication helps the other person understand what is on your mind. Being a good communicator requires expressing yourself, as well as active listening. Transposing the letters of listen yields silent. A good listener is quiet, yet engaged. After hearing the message, summarize it in your words to ensure you understood as intended. If your summary is incorrect, ask for clarification until you are on common ground...the root of communication. This technique allows you to sort through emotions to get to the heart of the message. When a person feels "heard," they tend to share more, thus opening the floodgates of improved communication.

Although communication is natural for me, many people with whom I interact struggle to express their thoughts and feelings. To ensure I convey my ideas accurately, regardless of the person or situation, I evaluate and then work to improve my communication skills. As the exchange requires, I invest time learning about the person's background and personality. I observe nonverbal cues that allow me to "read between the lines" to assess whether their actions contradict or complement their message.

God provided me with a model for interacting with people who have difficulty communicating. I am amazed at how well the conversation goes when I follow the leading of the Holy Spirit.

1. Ask God what He wants you to share with them. If it's a touchy subject, sometimes He instructs me to be quiet. Since the tongue is the deadliest member (James 3:8), take care in how you use it.

2. Anything you want to tell the person, tell it to God first. This strategy lets me express my feelings so the issue does not fester into bitterness. Hearing my words helps release the emotion tied to them and temper them so as not to offend my Abba.

3. Listen. Listen to His voice instruction. When I take "it" to Him first, He gives me insight into my delivery so I avoid overloading and/or overwhelming the receiver. It's like a practice run to work out the kinks.

4. Sometimes I write what I want to say in my journal. Telling them to God gets them out of my heart. Writing them gets them out of my head. With a cleared head and a pure heart, I can check my emotions, monitor my nonverbal actions, and stay in character. I communicate with confidence, clarity, and Christ.

5. During the conversation, the best way to gain insight into the other person's perspective is listening. Be mindful to listen to understand, not respond. God gave you two ears and one mouth, so listen twice as much as you speak.

A wise man will hear and increase learning, and a man of understanding will attain wise counsel,

— Proverbs 1:5

So then, my beloved brethren, let every man be swift to hear, slow to speak, slow to wrath;

—James 1:19

I was accused of not being a good communicator. God helped me not take the comment personally by separating the message from the messenger. He led me to conduct self-inventory to reflect on my role in the matter, then evaluate why the comment was made. Evaluating the whys allowed me to think about the conversation from their perspective. I discovered:

1. They did not like what I said
2. They did not understand what I said
3. I did not effectively communicate

When I have conversations with my wife, I am attentive to what she says. If the result is a honey-do list, I act on it as soon as possible. My immediate response shows her that I listened and understood.

When she feels heard, she is more willing to communicate with me.

Timing is Everything

Often, you will have to take the lead on communication. If she says that she is not ready, respect that. Don't take it personally if your wife doesn't want to talk when you do. The conversation flows better if you communicate when you are both willing to talk. Although it may be difficult to wait, especially when you perceive the matter is pressing, consider scheduling the conversation. Ask her for a specific time a day or two in advance or provide her with a couple of options. The delayed conversation allows time to manage emotions, consider options, and improve results.

Even when you have something good to share, if the timing is wrong, you may not get the response you hoped. For example, you're excited about a promotion. You meet your wife at the door to tell her about it. Her hands are filled with bags of groceries, the kids are tugging at her, and she sighs as she looks at the pile of dirty dishes stacked in the sink. Instead of overwhelming her with one more thing—albeit good—offer her time to decompress. Of course, you already grabbed the groceries, but take it a few steps further. Settle the kids, ask her if she would like a warm bubble bath, and then wash the dishes. I guarantee, when she finally hears your exciting news, she will respond with refreshed enthusiasm.

God's timing is best as He conditions her to receive your words. What you are telling her could be the same thing that you have tried to tell her in the past. What you were saying was not effective in the past because you were trying to tell her in your own timing and in your own way.

When the conversation happens, check in with her; otherwise, she may feel like you are shutting her out by dominating. Your goal is not to get things off your chest with the she-is-going-to-hear-me-or-else mentality. You want your wife to hear, understand, and respond. Conversations are dialogues, not monologues.

Many factors affect a message. The hidden gems shared in the next section can have a monumental effect on communication and overall quality of your relationship.

It's Not What You Say...Nonverbal Communication

The following content, provided by Valerie J. Lewis Coleman[2], describes the effect of nonverbal communication on a message.

Communication is an exchange through a common system of symbols that consists of explicit and implicit components. Explicit communication is the words that communicate facts and content. Implicit communication is the nonverbal content that expresses feeling and intent. This component amplifies the verbal message as it supports, modifies,

---

[2] *Nonverbal Communication* by Valerie J. Lewis Coleman of PenOfTheWriter.com. Sources: *How to Work With People*; Fred Pryor Corporate Training; *How to Communicate with Power and Confidence*; National Career Workshops; *Marketing* by Carl McDaniel, Jr. and William R. Darden.

or emphasizes the meaning of the words in one of six ways.

1. Repetition: Reinforces verbal communication through redundancy. For example, saying "okay" and gesturing it.

2. Contradiction: Opposes the message, such as a statement of sarcasm, "Sure, honey. I'm okay with more work. I have nothing better to do anyway."

3. Substitution: Attempts to create a nonverbal symbolic meaning in place of verbal communication like a hug to convey sympathy, a good-bye wave, or head nod.

4. Accentuation: Tone of message emphasizes what is being said. In a stern voice, your spouse says, "Come in the bedroom, right now!"

5. Complementary: Supplements and/or modifies the verbal message. For example, saying, "I love you," while holding hands, whispering, and gazing into her eyes.

6. Regulation: Helps control the flow of verbal interaction. This amplifier consists of body position, eye contact, vocal pitch, and touch.

A good listener will assess the nonverbal communication to determine the sincerity of a message because only seven percent of its meaning derives from words. Fifty-five percent of the meaning is nonverbal including body postures, gestures, and facial expressions. The remaining thirty-eight percent accounts for elements of sound: tempo, volume, tone, and silence.

The SOFTEN technique is a way to build rapport and enhance communication. The acronym means:

- **Smile**: sincere smile to decrease tension
- **Openness**: body posture with legs and arms uncrossed
- **Forward leaning**: shows interest
- **Touch**: a firm handshake or other nonsexual contact
- **Eye contact**: avoid staring, excessive blinking, or peering off into the distance

- **Names:** make a conscious effort to remember the name of everyone you meet

Remember:

- It's not what you say, but how you say it
- Actions speak louder than words
- Never let them see you sweat

Fair Fighting Rules

In the article, *30 Fair Fighting Rules for Couples*[3], the rules of engagement help ensure improved communication. To summarize 1 Corinthians 13:5, love does not dishonor others, is not self-seeking, is not easily angered, and keeps no record of wrongs. The following five rules resonate most with me because I implement them in my marriage and encourage my clients to do the same:

1. Don't fear conflict because fearing conflict causes you to avoid it. The result is matters

---

[3] *30 Fair Fighting Rules for Couples*, Psychologia.co online: https://psychologia.co/fair-fighting-rules (accessed September 27, 2018).

remain unresolved and fester like an open wound.

2. Being open about your needs and feelings allows you to express versus suppress your expectations.

3. Don't mention separation or divorce, which makes you susceptible to the enemy's divide-and-conquer tactic.

4. Don't keep score because the goal is win-win, not win-lose. Keeping score results in someone losing and devalues the relationship.

5. Keep your fights to yourself. Once you resolve the matter, outsiders often hold a grudge toward your partner. In addition, depending on their motives, they may intentionally give bad advice to cause more turmoil.

Read the full article and then commit to incorporate at least three rules into your marriage. Note that these rules are transferable to other relationship dynamics.

Education: The Great Equalizer

Many relational issues derive from not understanding the differences in how men and women communicate. Some fundamental differences[4] are:

- Women talk to vent emotions. Men are problem solvers who tend to talk to fix.

- Women prefer face-to-face conversations; whereas, men prefer shoulder-to-shoulder. At sporting events, fans sit shoulder-to-shoulder. When opposing players stand face-to-face, it is confrontational. On fishing trips, few words are spoken, fishers stand side-by-side and have a great experience, with or without catching fish. In war, shoulder-to-shoulder battle formations reinforce solidarity, comradery, and protection.

---

[4] *How Men and Women Differ: Gender Differences in Communication Styles, Influence Tactics, and Leadership Styles*, WTSNet.org online: https://wtsnet.org/wp-content/uploads/2018/02/How-Men-And-Women-Differ_-Gender-Differences-in-Communication-Sty.pdf (accessed October 6, 2020).

- Women tend to be right-brained which is where creativity, intuition, and emotions dominate. Most men are left-brained where logic, compartmentalization, and reasoning prevail. Compartmentalizing emotions allows soldiers to move past fear to fight on the frontline. This same trait explains how a man can have ongoing sex with a woman without having feelings for her.

These insights represent averages. As with any variable, outliers exist. The following sections delve into two significant differences that affect communication.

Love and Respect

Why did God command men to love their wives and wives to reverence (respect) their husbands? Because men thrive on respect like women thrive on love.

Nevertheless let each one of you in particular so love his own wife as himself, and let the wife see that she respects her husband.

—Ephesians 5:33

In his *New York Times* bestseller, *Love & Respect: The Love She Most Desires; The Respect He Desperately Needs*, Dr. Emerson Eggerichs explains how men and women are wired differently regarding love and respect. In any relationship dynamic, respect dominates for men. Not that love is not important, it's just a close second.

Consider a heated conversation between a man and a woman. As emotions flare, vicious words spew and hands flail. When she swivels her neck, rolls her eyes, or points her finger, he feels disrespected. Instead of becoming physical with the love of his life, as a man of integrity, he walks away. She deems his exit unloving and pursues him. They stand face-to-face with intensity that rivals volcanic eruptions. The more they interact, the more she feels unloved and he feels disrespected. They are on the "crazy cycle of love and respect" with no way off. Now consider the same heated conversation between two men. More than likely, the resolution would have ended with hand-to-hand combat.

Love Languages

When I conduct premarital counseling, I share how people tend to give love the way they want to receive it. Based on *The Five Love Languages* by Gary Chapman, arguments can be diffused — often before they start — just by understanding your mate's primary and secondary love language. In no particular order, the languages are

1. Quality Time: active engagement like board games, conversations, intimate dinners
2. Acts of Service: running errands, house chores
3. Words of Affirmation: compliments, verbal encouragement, affirmations
4. Gifts: store bought or handmade
5. Physical Touch: hand holding, kissing, sex

Read the book with your significant other and complete the quiz at https://www.5lovelanguages.com/quizzes. Learn her primary and secondary love languages, share yours with her, and then agree to express love for each other by honoring the stated heart's desires. If she needs love in a form that is unfamiliar to you, the adjustment may not be easy, but it will be well worth it.

When I shared with one couple how people tend to give love the way they want to receive it, they agreed that this difference was affecting their relationship. To prepare for the second session, I asked them to identify their primary and secondary love languages by completing the love language assessment. During the session, the wife shared that her primary love language was words of affirmation. The husband shared that his primary love language was quality time. The wife realized that while she was giving her husband compliments, he wanted quality time with her. The husband realized that affirming his wife with his words would fill her love tank. They made intentional efforts to give the other what they needed and not what they themselves wanted to receive. At the next session, they expressed their excitement with the shift in the marriage dynamic. Not only did each spouse feel loved, an added bonus was the satisfaction of knowing they made their spouse happier.

When I counsel couples, I stay connected with them for several months. For the six-month check-in, *Four Seasons of Marriage* by Gary Chapman is my preferred resource.

This book uses seasons to define the state of a marriage; noting that marriages do not necessarily follow chronological order. Winter marriages are cold, bitter, harsh, and isolated. Closeness is not found in a winter marriage. Spring marriages are filled with warm feelings like excitement, joy, hope, and happiness. Eros love is high in this season. Summer marriages are filled with fun and feelings of happiness, satisfaction, accomplishment, and connection. This marriage is the result of hard work invested during the spring stage. It is the pinnacle reflective of Cod's agapé love. A fall marriage appears fine on the outside; however, the inner workings are changing. This season is filled with sadness, apprehension, and rejection.

I use this book to help couples identify the season of their marriage and identify strategies to stay in the spring/summer seasons and get out of the winter/fall seasons.

I counseled a couple who identified their marriage as the spring season. Following the session, they were confident and committed to moving to the summer season.

Reflect

Describe your style of communication.

Who had the greatest effect on the way you communicate?

What situations make it difficult for you to communicate effectively?

What can you do to manage those situations *before* they occur?

What strategies have you implemented to become a better communicator?

Love Note to the Ladies

- ♥ Start the conversation by telling him if you want him to listen or provide a solution.
- ♥ Don't make him guess what you want and need. Tell him.

It's better to live alone in the corner of an attic than with a quarrelsome wife in a lovely home.

—Proverbs 25:24 New Living Translation

Chapter 2

God's Men Master Emotions

God has shown me how to better deal with situations by mastering my emotions. This skill allows me to be compassionate and sensitive to my wife's needs without falling apart. Since every situation is different, I seek God for guidance each time. By nature, I am not afraid or ashamed to express my feeling and cry when I am hurt. Since showing vulnerability has not always worked well for me, God helped me bridle my emotions.

When you lead with your emotions, you can be easily hurt. Sometimes, people perceive you as weak, which is why some men shy away from emotional situations. They are called insensitive if they don't show enough concern, or weak if they show too much. Since this catch-22 can be confusing, I choose to strive for meekness, which is strength under control. Let the Holy Spirit guide you in how to respond…the right way.

When you change your actions, don't expect people to change with you because maturity occurs at different rates. Be mindful not to revert to your old ways or become resentful if your attempts to be/do better aren't reciprocated. Don't do for others in the hopes that they will do the same for you; that's conditional love.

When you follow His lead, even if she is not pleased, God will be. Good emotional health is essential for healthy relationships to balance the highs and lows. If your emotions get too low, depression may follow. If you run on a consistent high, you may have difficulty handling disappointing situations or relating to others. Finding middle ground provides a solid foundation when the waves crash and bask in the sunlight.

Managing emotions improved relationships with my family. I am more aware of how my actions can have lasting effects on them: positive or negative. My responsibility is to help my family have healthy emotions as well. Emotions can be complex and sometimes difficult to communicate, so be patient.

Ephesians 6:10-18 describes the armor of God that prepares and protects from the fiery darts of the enemy. Verse 14 refers to the "belt of truth" that I simulate putting on before having a difficult conversation as my reminder to keep my emotions in check.

> *Stand therefore, having girded your waist*
> *with truth, having put on the breastplate of*
> *righteousness,*
> —Ephesians 6:14

God cannot use me when I let my flesh (emotions) take the lead. God is an emotional God who loves, hates, and gets angry; however, He does not act irrational or sporadic in response to you. Thank God! He is concerned about your emotions, but He is more concerned about your character and reaction to situations. Mastering emotions allows you to mimic Jesus and attempt to respond the way He would. You cannot be Jesus, but you can be like Him. Because you were made in His image.

Reflect

In your relationship, who is more emotional: you or your wife? Why?

What are your emotional triggers?

What do you do when you become emotional?

Have you seen good examples of men who master their emotions? Explain.

Love Note to the Ladies

♥ Allow your husband to express his emotions in his own way without criticism or judgment.

♥ Do not take his display of emotions as weakness.

♥ Take care in how you speak to your husband. Although he may never admit it, it takes longer to get over hurtful words from you than anyone else.

Chapter 3

God's Men Commit

Not all men are commitment phobic. In fact, men love to commit to value. Being slow to commit is often a result of

1. Wondering if a better option is available
2. Being unclear about the details of the commitment
3. Being unwilling to deal with the stuff that comes with commitment

Some women have experienced so much hurt and betrayal that they will not let you get close to their heart. They put up a wall thinking that it protects them by keeping you out. Some women don't know who they are, so trying to connect on an intimate, nonsexual way is almost impossible. Since men can see warning signs, yielding to commitment is an innate defense mechanism.

Like communication, commitment is a balancing act. When one party expects more than they are willing to give, the relationship suffers. You cannot expect fine dining, with a fast-food mentality. Reciprocity makes for a solid relationship.

Seek God when deciding whether to commit to a relationship. If it takes a while to hear from Him, you may risk being labeled a man who does not commit, but do not move without God's instruction. If He does not want you to commit to the relationship, do not leave her dangling in uncertainty. Tell her that you do not want to commit, and then avoid words or actions that can mislead her to think otherwise.

Before committing to a woman, first commit to God. Your commitment to learning, understanding and walking with God is preparation for communing with your wife. How can you love her as Christ loves the church, if you don't know the depth of His agapé (unconditional) love?

Husbands, love your wives, just as Christ also loved the church and gave Himself for her.

—Ephesians 5:25

Commitment to Christ is another brick in the foundation of a strong marriage, which is holy, sacred, and important to God. It is a covenant—or binding contract—between God, husband, and wife symbolizing the strength of the Trinity. "A powerful supernatural energy is released when the three 'cords' work together in perfect unity to effect the divine will."[5]

Though one may be overpowered by another, two can withstand him. And a threefold cord is not quickly broken.

—Ecclesiastes 4:12

---

[5] *A Threefold Cord Reflects the Power of the Trinity,* TruthImmutable.com online: http://truthimmutable.com/threefold-cord-reflects-power-trinity (accessed April 6, 2020).

My father was a good example of family commitment. If he got home before my mother, which was often the case, he cooked dinner. He shopped for groceries to lessen mom's workload. He was committed to our wellbeing until he died in 1991 at 43 years old. Directly and indirectly, I learned skills necessary to be a good husband and father. My father sacrificed for us and as I matured, I realized just how much. He made sure that my sister and I had money for extra-curricular activities even when he was not working. I was a three-sport athlete in high school, but no matter where my games occurred, my father was there.

When God blessed me with my family, I pulled from his example. Without thinking about it, I did things for them. Not only did I provide financially, I provided spiritual direction, emotional support, and plenty of love, affection, and attention. I gave them me. I attended football games, track meets, and cheerleading events. When my children had academic achievements and recognitions, I was there. From kindergarten through high school, I attended open houses, and met with teachers for parent-teacher meetings. I wanted their teachers to know they had a committed father.

Reflect

What does it mean to you to be committed in a relationship?

Who had the greatest influence on how you commit? Why?

What makes it easy for you to commit?

What makes it difficult for you to commit?

Love Note to the Ladies

♥ Before accusing your mate of not wanting to commit, have a conversation with him. Using the when-you-I-feel-because model, express your concerns and allow him to respond. For example, when you shut down, I feel alone because I need emotional attachment with you.

♥ Understand that "not right now" does not mean never. Men often need time to process information before answering especially as it pertains to difficult situations.

Chapter 4

God's Men Nurture

Because men are instinctively protective, nurturing requires more effort. By God's design, women are naturally more nurturing than men. Compounded with nine months of gestation, it's no wonder provision and protection don't automatically create nurturing qualities.

From a male perspective, nurturing is active involvement in educating and rearing the children. It is not enough to be present and provide. Nurturing men are emotionally in tune with their children to help develop their character.

During each of our three pregnancies, I talked to the fetuses. I wanted my children to hear my voice and know I was present. To further establish a bond, during the deliveries I held each child before cutting the umbilical cord.

As a nurturer, I cater to the needs of my children. I know their individual personalities and purposely customize the love and care necessary to meet their unique needs. Since a father is a daughter's first love and a son's first hero, I am chivalrous toward my daughters. I open doors for them, greet/depart with a hug and kiss on the cheek, and tell them that I love them. As my son's hero, I show him that real men love God first and are responsible for their actions. My son doesn't always get a kiss on the cheek, but I hug him as a public display of affection.

My son modeled his behavior after mine. By witnessing our behavior, my daughters know that men can be nurturers.

My prayer is that my actions help my children choose well-rounded, quality spouses. Children reap the benefits of parents who nurture them. In my experience, they tend to have high self-esteem and confidence and are more expressive about their feelings, showing love and receiving it.

Your sons need to know that men can be nurturing to help develop this trait before they get caught up in what the world says they should be: emotionless, detached, and abrasive. No one should have your children's attention more than you. Pastors, teachers, and coaches should reinforce what you have already taught them. Young men need to learn how to balance strength with nurturing. As for daughters, when they experience a nurturing father, they are more likely to expect similar affection from the men they date. Children are master mimics, so lead by example.

When it comes to nurturing my wife, I give her the same attention and affection given to my daughters plus more. If she needs to cry, I offer my shoulders. If she needs to vent about her work day, I listen. I can recognize when she is hurting and without being asked, I rub her feet, or prepare a hot bath to help alleviate her stress.

Reflect

What benefits does nurturing provide?

Were you nurtured as a child?

If yes, did you receive nurturing from you mother, father or both parents?

Do you consider yourself a good nurturer? Why or why not?

Love Note to the Ladies

♥ If your husband is not nurturing you the way you desire, tell him. Don't make him guess or assume what you want and need. If your husband does not respond when you tell him what you want or need, then write him a letter. Share how you feel when he doesn't give you what you want or need and how you feel when he does. Give him examples of how you responded when you got what you wanted or needed to illustrate the cause-and-effect of his actions. By writing, you work through your feelings and disconnect the emotion from the message.

Chapter 5

God's Men Apologize

Not all men have a problem apologizing. Responsible men realize that apologizing is not a display of weakness, but rather acknowledging a mistake, mishap, or misunderstanding and attempting to correct it. A person will not try to get something right if they don't feel like they have done something wrong. Offering an apology shows that you are concerned about the relationship and your standing with God.

When I make a parenting mistake, I confess it to my children. This admission lets them know that it is okay to make mistakes, and more importantly, the protocol for righting the wrong. Without your example, your children may have a difficult time admitting an error.

The challenge with apologizing is not expecting an apology in return. Whether the recipient doesn't feel they wronged you or they are unwilling/unable to extend one to you, apologize anyway. Your wife and children need to see that you are willing to make amends by clearing the atmosphere of negativity, committing to changing the behavior and then actively working to do so. Apologizing helps fulfill God's command:

If it is possible, as far as it depends on you, live at peace with everyone.

—Romans 12:18

Then Peter came to Him and said, "Lord, how often shall my brother sin against me, and I forgive him? Up to seven times?"
Jesus said to him, "I do not say to you, up to seven times, but up to seventy times seven."

—Matthew 18:21-22

Since apologies and forgiveness go hand-in-hand, the next chapter delves into the benefits of forgiveness and the consequences of avoiding it.

Reflect

Did you have a role model to show you the importance of apologizing?

Is it difficult for you to apologize?

If so, what makes it difficult?

Do you perceive apologizing as weakness?

Love Note to the Ladies

♥ When your husband apologizes, be careful not to make him feel weak or embarrassed. Because men do not like to feel vulnerable, he will avoid future apologies.

Whoever loves instruction loves
knowledge, but he who hates
correction is stupid.
A good man obtains favor from the
Lord, but a man of wicked intentions
He will condemn.
A man is not established by
wickedness, but the root of the
righteous cannot be moved.
—Proverbs 12:1-3

Chapter 6

God's Men Forgive

Holding onto unforgiveness affects your relationship with God. When you've been abandoned, betrayed, or disappointed, it's easy to distance yourself from the offender physically, yet hold on to the emotional wounds. If unaddressed, anger can settle in your heart shifting to bitterness and ultimately, revenge.

> *Beloved, do not avenge yourselves, but rather give place to wrath; for it is written, "Vengeance is Mine, I will repay," says the Lord.*
> —Romans 12:19

So what is a healthy alternative to revenge? Forgiveness, which is essential in this Christian walk. No question that you will be offended. With respect to your wife, the strain worsens because you must interact to manage money, children, and other family matters. Without forgiveness, putting your heart into what you are doing is a challenge.

It is hard to forgive someone who does not feel like they did anything that warrants forgiveness or is not willing to apologize. Have you ever questioned, "How can she expect me to do things for her when she has not apologized?" I have. Don't let her actions shift your reaction to negativity by sulking or ignoring her in an attempt to manipulate a response. Instead, let the Holy Spirit lead you to do the right thing. I do not recommend ignoring her; however, silence is a powerful tool. It helps to deescalate a situation—no fuel, no fire—grants time to process your thoughts, and positions you to hear God. Silence is not giving in or condoning her actions, but rather concern about how being disobedient affects your relationship with Christ. Using silence as a weapon to exert power over someone or create emotional distance is abusive. The person on the receiving end of the silent treatment might feel ostracized, abandoned, and bullied, which can trigger childhood or relational traumas.

Modeling Forgiveness

Serving publishing clients to experience inner peace through forgiveness, Valerie J. Lewis Coleman[6] provided the following information:

Matters left unresolved grow in the heart like a deep-rooted weed causing resentfulness, bitterness, and physical ailments. Forgiveness transforms anger and hurt into healing and peace. Forgiveness can help you overcome depression, anxiety, and rage. Forgiveness gives you the power to resolve personal and relational conflicts. When you make a conscious decision to release a grudge, hurt, or disappointment, you take control, stand in your power, and own your worth. Forgiveness is not for the other person, but yourself as every mistake has within it an opportunity for you to grow, mature, and improve.

---

[6] *Pen of the Writer Mentoring: Forgiveness* provided by Valerie J. Lewis Coleman of PenOfTheWriter.com.

Use the following protocol and prayer to bring healing to your mind, body and soul:

7 Protocols of Forgiveness[7]

1. Thank God for forgiving you for those offenses you committed knowingly and unknowingly.

2. Ask God, "Who do I need to forgive and for what?" Sit quiet and listen.

3. Repent of your sin of unforgiveness. Don't let your ego (pride) get you in trouble. Recognize your wrong, admit it, and ask Him for forgiveness.

4. Forgive each offender and offense from your heart.

   "Lord, I choose to forgive _____ from my heart for _____. Lord, is there anything else for which I need to forgive _____? I declare _____ is no longer in my debt.

---

[7] *7 Protocols of Forgiveness* provided by Darnyelle Jervey Harmon of IncredibleOneEnterprises.com at Breakthrough in Business May 2018.

_____ is no longer taking up energy and space in my life."

5. Ask God to bless them and look for ways to bless them, when possible.

    "Lord, I release _____ to Your highest good."

6. Commit to "not remember" the offense. If/When the memory returns, say

    "I don't know why this memory is here. I specifically remember forgiving that. God, I thank You for the freedom forgiveness brought me. I bless _____ and release him/her/it to Your greater good. Father, I ask for Your divine reconciliation and I resolve to have no more emotional attachment to _____."

7. Make pre-forgiveness a lifestyle. Don't put yourself in situations to have to forgive. Ask God for discernment to avoid future incidents. Recite my prayer of forgiveness daily.

Prayer of Forgiveness

Father, in Matthew 6:14-15, You said that I must forgive others before You will forgive me. I choose to release all the pain and hurt that others have caused me and forgive them. I commit to forgiving myself for offenses I committed — intentional or unintentional — toward You, others, and myself. Father, thank You for forgiving me, teaching me how to forgive, and replacing the pain with Your unconditional love. In the matchless name of Jesus, amen.

Reflect

Whom do you need to forgive?

When was the last time you forgave yourself?

What process do you use to forgive?

How do you know when you have forgiven someone?

Love Note to the Ladies

- ♥ Don't attempt to force forgiveness from your husband. Allow him to offer forgiveness in his own way.

- ♥ Be mindful that forgiveness is not synonymous with weakness.

A soft answer turns away wrath, but a
harsh word stirs up anger. The tongue
of the wise uses knowledge rightly, but
the mouth of fools pours forth
foolishness.
The eyes of the Lord are in every place,
keeping watch on the evil and the
good.
—Proverbs 15:1-3

Chapter 7

God's Men are Romantic

Real men know romance is way more than sex. It's easy to become discouraged when your romantic gestures are not received as hoped; however, instead of letting frustration win, try something new. Ask her what she likes, wants, and needs from you. Be intentional with things that sweep her off her feet.

Romance differs from sex because it taps into emotions. It is a sensitive and intimate way of expressing how much you love your partner. Romance, which causes you to open up and be vulnerable, is selfless; sex is selfish. Without romance, sex is only a physical release.

One romantic idea is to plan an intimate dinner or game night with the objective of understanding and ranking her love languages. Take the guesswork out of romance by giving her what she wants. Yes, the spontaneity is gone...initially. However, as you develop a repertoire of chivalrous acts to which she favorably responds, you can re-introduce — or introduce — spontaneous gestures.

I learned this lesson by first-hand experience. I assumed doing for my wife what I wanted her to do for me would make us both happy. I was wrong.

Physical touch is my primary love language, so I would sit next to my wife and attempt to hold her hand. She felt smothered and did not respond to my efforts in like manner. Since quality time is my secondary love language, I planned things for us to do together. However, the spontaneity was not always well-received because she had other things planned.

God showed me that He wired her differently. I had to check my emotions so I didn't resent my wife's responses. I now know that I can't change my wife, nor do I want to anymore.

Romance is stimulating my wife's emotions by giving her what she wants without intercourse. I rub her feet, massage her, coordinate a picnic lunch to break up her work day, and walk on the beach holding hands. I love to prepare candle-light dinners, place a rose on her pillow, feed her fruit in the bed, and write poetry for her. I learned that my wife is romanced most by dressing up for dinner at a quaint tea house.

At times, she tells me that she appreciates my romantic efforts. Other times, I observe her change in mood. She becomes more talkative when she is relaxed and romanced.

Sex cannot be the expected end of romance; otherwise, your wife may assume you have ulterior motives.

Reflect

What does romance mean to you?

Do you consider yourself romantic? Why or why not?

What does romance mean to your wife?

Do you consider your wife romantic? Why or why not?

Love Note to Ladies

- ♥ Show him how you want to be romanced until it becomes natural for him.

- ♥ Be specific with your wants, needs, and expectations.

Chapter 8

God's Men are Sexual

A healthy sex life is important in marriage. If physical touch is not important to your wife, approach lovemaking delicately. If you are pushy, she may feel that your only objective is sex without concern for her or how she feels.

People in healthy relationships do not keep score or track who does something better. Ask God to help you not feel like you are competing with your wife. You are not losing when your wife gets what she wants. Sex is not about keeping score, which ultimately results in a win-lose situation. Your goal is a win-win outcome. Lovemaking must be mutually agreed upon before it is enjoyed the way that God intended.

God's Plan for Sex in Marriage

The Bible is filled with love stories and references to how marriage is to be a reflection of God's love.

"The Song of Songs is a collection of ancient Israelite love poems that celebrates the beauty and power of God's gift of love and sexual desire."[8] Also referred to as Song of Solomon, this book has poetic cycles that focus on the mystery and gift of sexual love.

> Now concerning the things whereof ye wrote unto me: It is good for a man not to touch a woman. Nevertheless, to avoid fornication, let every man have his own wife, and let every woman have her own husband. Let the husband render unto the wife due benevolence: and likewise also the wife unto the husband. The wife hath not power of her own body, but the husband: and likewise also the husband hath not

8 *Song of Songs,* BibleProject.com online: https://bibleproject.com/explore/song-of-songs (Accessed October 29, 2020).

power of his own body, but the wife. Defraud ye not one the other, except it be with consent for a time, that ye may give yourselves to fasting and prayer; and come together again, that Satan tempt you not for your incontinency.

—1 Corinthians 7:1-5

To honor each other, the husband and wife must remain faithful to the marriage covenant. God will judge those who commit adultery or withhold sex to manipulate their mate.

Marriage is honorable in all, and the bed undefiled: but whoremongers and adulterers God will judge.

—Hebrews 13:4

The only competition in your marriage is competing to see who loves God and spouse most. Complement, not compete.

Since men are visually stimulated, responses to your wife's body may make her feel that sex is always on your mind. A study conducted by Ohio State University[9] found that men think about sex 19 times a day, which is almost twice that of women who think about sex 10 times day.

The frequency of thinking about sex and having it varies considerably. Although it is never good to compare your sex life with others, understanding averages brings balance to expectations. According to Very Well Mind[10], on average, married couples have sex once a week with emphasis on quality and quantity.

Multiple factors affect desire including mutual respect, emotional health, and everyday demands. If

---

[9] *Health Myth: Do Men Really Think about Sex Every 7 Seconds?*, GQ.com online: https://www.gq.com/story/health-myth-does-the-average-man-really-think-about-sex-every-7-seconds/amp (Accessed April 15, 2020).
[10] *What Marital Sex Statistics Can Reveal*, VeryWellMind.com online: https://www.verywellmind.com/what-marital-sex-statistics-can-reveal-2300946 (Accessed April 15, 2020).

you and your wife are unable—or unwilling—to satisfy each other's sexual desires,

1. Talk to God. He intended sex to be enjoyed, not tolerated.

2. Talk to each other. Although it may sound stoic, scheduling sex can help alleviate tension.

3. Talk to a professional counselor. Working with an unbiased third party can reveal underlying issues that influence communication, sex, parenting, and more.

Withholding sex attempting to change behavior is a weapon of mass manipulation. On the other extreme, rewarding behaviors with sex can create false expectations. Sex is an expression of love that is psychological, emotional, and physical.

Reflect

What does being sexual mean to you?

How do you show your wife that you are ready for sex?

Have you ever talked with your wife about sexual compatibility?

What are her expectations for sex?

Love Note to Ladies

♥ Be careful not to use sex to manipulate your husband. Whether rewarding him for a job well done or punishing him for unsatisfactory performance, God did not create sex as a form of payment or torment.

Chapter 9

God's Men Multitask

Although the verdict is still out on who is better at multitasking, studies have cited several factors that may affect it.

- Experience[11]. The more you do something, the easier it becomes. When combined with another task, the routine task functions on automatic pilot.

- Order of tasks. Activities completed in sequential order are easier to manage than those done simultaneously.[12]

---

[11] *Are Women Better at Multitasking than Men?*, UU.nl online: https://www.uu.nl/en/organisation/faculty-of-social-and-behavioural-sciences/are-women-better-at-multitasking-than-men (Accessed 16, 2020).

[12] *Are Women Better at Multitasking than Men?*, BioMedCentral.com online: https://bmcpsychology.biomedcentral.com/articles/10.1186/2050-7283-1-18 (Accessed April 16, 2020).

- Hormonal differences may give women a slight edge.[13]
- The corpus callosum is a bridge of nerve endings that connects the brain's right and left hemispheres. For women, the bridge tends to be 30% more developed allowing information to flow easier and faster.[14]

Regardless of who science says is better, multitasking is essential to master work-life balance.

My first two children are only two years apart. When they were younger, they required lots of care and attention, often at the same time. One wanted to play ball while the other needed to be fed or changed. I cooked since my wife worked during the day. I

---

[13] *Scientists May Have Proven Woman are Better at Multitasking than Men*, TheConversation.com online: https://theconversation.com/scientists-may-have-proven-women-are-better-at-multitasking-than-men-71877 (Accessed April 16, 2020).

[14] *Are Women Better at Multitasking than Men?*, TechRepublic.com online: https://www.techrepublic.com/blog/career-management/are-women-better-at-multitasking-than-men (Accessed April 16, 2020).

worked the night shift. We shared household chores, some of which many considered "wifely" duties.

I am thankful God showed me how to develop a system. As the children aged, they got involved in more activities. To keep up with their full schedules, I posted the weekly itinerary on the refrigerator and reviewed it daily. On my way home, I called to make sure they completed homework, ate a snack, and had their athletic equipment ready. At times, I helped one daughter with homework, got my son ready for football practice, and cooked dinner. When my youngest daughter started cheering, I moved from child-to-child like a back-and-forth Wimbledon tennis tournament. I listened as each child recounted their day. Between the three of them, they always had lots to share.

Effective multitasking also helps me at work. I supervise a team of three retirement planners who travel the state conducting workshops and counseling teachers preparing to retire. An average day at work requires me to juggle tasks like coordinating schedules, confirming travel reservations, assigning projects, and addressing escalated client matters. Since I do the same type of work as my team, multitasking ensures we are successful individually and collectively.

God added another exciting responsibility to my life: pastor. My weekly routine includes family commitments, the day job, preparing and preaching Sunday sermons, creating and teaching Bible study lessons, and being available for church members would all be next to impossible without God and multitasking. He gives me power to balance spiritual, familial, pastoral, and vocational responsibilities infused with recreational time in the gym to stay physically fit for this demanding schedule.

Reflect

What does multitasking look like for you?

Are you good at it?

As a child, did you have a good example of multitasking? Explain.

Love Note to Ladies

- ♥ Recognize your husband's efforts to multitask.

- ♥ Understand that his multitasking will probably differ from yours...not wrong, just different.

The preparations of the heart belong to
man, but the answer of the tongue is
from the Lord.
All the ways of a man are pure in his
own eyes, but the Lord weighs the
spirits.
Commit your works to the Lord, and
your thoughts will be established.
— Proverbs 16:1-3

Chapter 10

God's Men Support and Understand

Because God wired me differently — committed to my family, communicative of my feelings, and consistent with my forgiveness — I often felt unsupported, lonely, and frustrated. Following the divorce from my wife, I did not want to hear or see anything about relationships. I changed TV channels if I saw a couple holding hands. When a romantic song played on the radio, I turned it off. Not that I was against marriage, but I longed for support and understanding. I needed my love tank filled.

My relationship with God grew from the loneliness. I spent more time talking — and listening — to Him. He showed me new aspects of my relationships, why my wife reacted like she did and what to do about it. He encouraged me to love my wife as He loves the church (Ephesians 5). He mandated that I am responsible for sharing my healing process with men who need support and understanding about not feeling heard by the wife, and then charged me with being a good example for my children.

Although it may not be easy, know that God rewards your obedience. Whether you get the results you hoped, your obedience blesses your wife and you while providing a model for your children to emulate. They learn unconditional love through you.

Marriage is not 50/50, 70/30, or 80/20. God expects 100/100 all the time. Several Scriptures reveal God's plan for husband and wife to become one.

> *Therefore a man shall leave his father and mother and be joined to his wife, and they shall become one flesh.*
> —Genesis 2:24

> *And the two shall become one flesh; so then they are no longer two, but one flesh.*

— Mark 10:8

*"For this reason a man shall leave his father
and mother and be joined to his wife, and
the two shall become one flesh."*

— Ephesians 5:31

Just as God is a God of multiplication as noted in
the parable of talents (Matthew 25:14-30), 30, 60, 100-
fold blessings (Matthew 13:8), and two putting 10,000
to flight (Deuteronomy 32:30), marriage is
multiplicative.

Chapter 11 of *The Forbidden Secrets of the Goody
Box*[15] illustrates how marriage attaches you to in-
laws, exes, and tons of life experiences that can affect
the relationship dynamic. Looking at two-become-
one-flesh Scriptures (Genesis 2:24, Mark 10:8-10; 1
Corinthians 6:16; 1 Peter 3:7) from a mathematical

---

[15] *The Forbidden Secrets of the Goody Box – Relationship Advice
That Your Father Didn't Tell You and Your Mother Didn't
Know* by Valerie J. Lewis Coleman.
TheGoodyBoxBook.com.

perspective, the only way two can become one is by multiplying: one man times one woman equals one flesh. You cannot bring together two half-people (broke, bruised, and broken) and produce a whole relationship. A fulfilling relationship requires that both the man and woman are whole.

Everyone has times when they're not at their best; however, if the imbalance occurs for an extended period, address it. Have a conversation and if necessary, get professional help. It is critical to find an unbiased third party to express your marital concerns. Don't bottle up these matters hoping they will magically work out on their own. Like a small cut, issues left unattended can fester into infection, gangrene, and amputation. If your wife refuses to go to counselling, then go alone. You will acquire strategies to use when you interact with your wife. With consistency, she will see your subtle changes and may desire to experience more by attending counseling.

Though tempting, don't share your problems with another woman unless she's a professional counselor hired to help your marriage. Otherwise, you run the risk of developing an emotional attachment with her, which could lead to isolation from your wife and ultimately, an affair. If your church doesn't have a men's ministry, your pastor may be a good confidante assuming his commitments allow.

God wired me to be a prayer warrior, worshiper, provider, and protector for my family. I strive toward the calling God placed on my life with a spirit of excellence and love. I serve a perfect God whose strength is made perfect in my weakness.

> *And He said to me, "My grace is sufficient for you, for My strength is made perfect in weakness." Therefore most gladly I will rather boast in my infirmities, that the power of Christ may rest upon me.*
> —2 Corinthians 12:9

Not that I walk around euphoric every day, but God taught me how to live in love.

*And above all things have fervent love for
one another, for love will cover a multitude
of sins.*

—1 Peter 4:8

Allowing love to cover a person's sin is not condoning the sin. You just don't hold the sin against the person.

I had the privilege of meeting men who felt the same way I do: uncomfortable with society's negative labeling of men. Men have been conditioned to believe that talking about life issues was a sign of weakness. Most behaviors are taught (direct influence) or caught (indirect influence). Caught behaviors are learned by observation and when good examples are not present to model, bad habits form.

Man of God, take your rightful place. Know that God hears you and He is concerned about you in every aspect.

For I know the thoughts that I think toward
you, says the Lord, thoughts of peace and
not of evil, to give you a future and a hope.
—Jeremiah 29:11

Everything that happens in your life is for your good and God's glory. In some situations, you can immediately see the good. Other situations require faith, trust, and time to understand the lesson God embedded in them.

And we know that all things work together
for good to those who love God, to those who
are the called according to His purpose.
—Romans 8:28

One thing my experiences taught me is unconditional love. I knew how to love a person who loved me the way I wanted, but God showed me how to love people even when they don't love me in return. How? By choosing to focus on His expectations of me and not their response to me.

Regardless of how my wife acted, I was responsible for loving her the way God commanded...without condition. If you don't love your wife unconditionally, you are being disobedient to God and damaging your relationship with Him. Everything you do, do it as though you are doing it for God.

You are responsible for teaching your sons and other men God's plan for men. It is not okay to mimic the world because you can't get anyone to understand or accept you. This race is not about acceptance. Your purpose is pleasing God. Don't be afraid to admit that you need help. As Les Brown said, "Ask for help. Not because you are weak, but because you want to remain strong."

> *But Moses' hands became heavy; so they took a stone and put it under him, and he sat on it. And Aaron and Hur supported his hands, one on one side, and the other on the other side; and his hands were steady until the going down of the sun. So Joshua*

defeated Amalek and his people with the
edge of the sword.
—Exodus 17:12-13

With the help of his network, Moses fulfilled his God-mandated assignment and Joshua defeated the enemy. What if Moses was too proud to ask for help or unwilling to accept it? What if Aaron or Hur refused to offer support: moral, physical, or otherwise? What if Joshua commanded his army to run versus relying on Moses?

Keep your brothers lifted in prayer. Support them with time, money, and encouraging words.

As iron sharpens iron, so a man sharpens
the countenance of his friend.
—Proverbs 27:17

Ask God what His purpose is for you, and then develop a vision statement to keep you focused. Speak your statement aloud twice a day: first thing in the morning to start your day and before bed to reflect upon while sleeping.

> *Where there is no vision, the people perish:*
> *but he that keepeth the law, happy is he.*
> —Proverbs 29:18 KJV

> *Then the Lord answered me and said:*
> *"Write the vision and make it plain on*
> *tablets, that he may run who reads it."*
> —Habakkuk 2:2

God gave me the following vision statement years ago:

> I will be true to God, my family, and myself. I will be filled with, and led by, the Holy Spirit. I will share what I have and what I know. I will never stop seeking God's wisdom and knowledge.

Developing this statement helped me identify areas that I focus on daily. It also helps me avoid conforming to someone else's vision for me. I assess myself to see if I am being who God called me to be. I put Him first and follow His commands, convictions, and covenant.

> *All the paths of the Lord are mercy and truth, to such as keep His covenant and His testimonies.*
> —Psalms 25:10

I stay in communion with God to fulfill my purpose. I am true to my family by living the Word, feeding the Word to them, and acting on the Word in my interaction with them. I don't want my family questioning my integrity — at home or the pulpit — by saying, "How can he tell men to do things for their families that he is not doing for his own?" I want them to see a sermon in me, not just hear one from me. Daily, I ask God to fill me with His Spirit for revelation knowledge and wisdom to make sound decisions. I do what He tells me to do. I share by giving, preaching, and teaching.

Oftentimes, when you are not living up to God's plan for you, you may become angry because things are more difficult. Conforming to your spouse or society will not necessarily keep the peace and make things better, especially when out of God's will. The danger of going along with what society says can make you numb to a situation. You may not respond in an attempt to avoid chaos at home. How many times have you heard, "If mama is happy, the whole house is happy" or "happy wife, happy life" or" happy spouse, happy house"? These statements may be true on the surface, but they are not biblical. If your efforts to make "mama" happy are not rooted in the Word, they will not last. How long would you work for an employer—without a paycheck—before you become bitter and resentful? What happens when you perform at your peak only to be skipped over for the promotion? Would you sabotage equipment, destroy property, or walk away?

Your efforts do not always yield the expected results especially when you operate in God's permissive will. Because He is a gentle, loving God who wants you to choose righteousness, you have freewill. This gift to humanity is the root cause of destructive lifestyles, so He cushioned it with grace. Grace to endure self-inflicted situations from the cross to which you nailed yourself. Like teaching a child to ride a bike by allowing them to have a guided fall, He permits your choices and actions; however, His preference is that you operate in His perfect will, which is His purpose and plan for you. When you reside in His perfect will, you receive all that He has for you, in His time.

If you tolerate selfishness, stubbornness, and disrespect, your family will assume it is acceptable to act contrary to God's will and you are guilty of helping them. The longer this behavior occurs, the harder to correct it. Set the tone for your household using God as the benchmark. Take the lead as influencer for your family. You are the priest of your home, not your pastor. Conceding your influence to someone else can be catastrophic. Your children may grow to resent you and your wife may lose respect for you.

Let the Holy Spirit develop Christ-like character in you by walking in the fruit of the Spirit.

> *But the fruit of the Spirit is love, joy, peace, longsuffering, kindness, goodness, faithfulness, gentleness, self-control. Against such there is no law.*
> —Galatians 5:22-23

I pray for God to help me with my own situations. He revealed to me that the difficulty in my marriage is the cross to carry.

> *Then He said to them all, "If anyone desires to come after Me, let him deny himself, and take up his cross daily, and follow Me.*
> —Luke 9:23

Cross carrying is difficult especially when you carry the same cross year after year. Seek God always, particularly when you feel overwhelmed. The longer you wait to go to the throne, the more chances the devil has to bombard you with negative thoughts. More than likely, the situation will not change overnight, but don't give up on God. He has not forgotten you. No matter how heavy the load, do not quit.

When considering your cross, don't try to carry the cross meant for your wife. Taking on someone else's responsibility stifles their growth while adding undue stress on yourself. Cover her daily in prayer, but do not carry her cross. As a natural protector, it is easy to enable her and get in God's way. Discern if you are protecting, preventing, or prying. God loves her more than you do. He knows what's best for her and your children.

Although I teach my children, God showed me that I have to approach my wife from a different mindset. When I communicate with my wife, my message is better received when I share with her as a peer versus trying to teach her like a student.

As a man, you tend to think about your family's needs before your own. God revealed to me that when it comes to provision and protection, my family comes first; however, regarding correction, I must start with myself. Take constant inventory of yourself. Spend time in the Word, pray daily, and ask Him to expose your weaknesses and vulnerabilities. Use His insight to guide you to be the best man you can. We must remember that the original covenant God made was with man.

You should not base your actions on your family's appreciation. If you follow the Holy Spirit and set a precedent, your family might not understand, but they will know that you care and have their best interest in mind. Your motivation must be your desire to be obedient to Christ. Be intentional about teaching your children and sharing with your wife. When you set a solid foundation for your family, they get it, even when you don't think they do. Indirectly, you create generational blessings with lessons, tools, and examples that can be shared with your lineage for years to come.

Reflect

Do you know what God's will is for you?

What does support from your wife look like to you?

Have you ever tried to carry your wife's cross?

What does it mean to cover your wife's sins?

How do you show your wife unconditional love?

Love Note to Ladies

♥ When your husband asks for help, don't use it against him later in an argument.

Better is a dry morsel with quietness,
than a house full of feasting with strife.
— Proverbs 17:1

Chapter 11

God's Men Stick and Stay

When things are not going well in your marriage, stick and stay. Beyond not getting your way, your wife shutting down paradise, or going through the motions to keep peace, stick and stay. When you feel like you are giving more than you are getting, stick and stay. You will experience some of the same things as non-believers, but you are expected to handle them differently. Learn to respond and not react. A reaction is often immediate, without much thought, and aggressive. A response is thought out, calm, and non-threatening. Handling situations differently, does not mean that they do not have the same effect on you.

How can you love your wife as Christ loved the church according to Ephesians 5:25, when she is not loving or respectful? Seek God, stand on His promises and stay in the marriage.

The Bible is clear that a husband-and-wife team are most effective when they work together.

> *Two are better than one; because they have a good reward for their labor. For if they fall, the one will lift up his fellow: but woe to him that is alone when he falleth; for he hath not another to help him up. Again, if two lie together, then they have heat: but how can one be warm alone? And if one prevail against him, two shall withstand him; and a threefold cord is not quickly broken.*
>
> —Ecclesiastes 4:9-12

Do not ignore your wife, but do not focus all your attention on her. Follow God and do not react negatively when she does something that displeases you. God sees everything you experience. Claim Him as El Roi (God Who Sees). Not all men shut down, even when it is tempting to do so. As God works on your wife, don't become resentful and treat her with hostility. Communicate your feelings. Ask God to condition her heart to receive what you are saying. A person will not change their mind if their will has not changed.

Your wife's background and upbringing affect how she responds to you. Some women think that men should "just deal with it." They assume that men are not supposed to hurt or show emotions. This logic is dangerous because it will cause you to hold in your feelings or share them with someone other than your wife. Containing your feelings can cause you to explode or implode. Sharing with the wrong person can lead you down a rabbit hole of regret. If you must share, find a trustworthy brother in Christ in whom you can confide. Seek wise counsel from a nonjudgmental person who is passionate about seeing your marriage thrive.

> *A wise man will hear and increase learning,*
> *and a man of understanding will attain*
> *wise counsel.*
> —Proverbs 1:5

We all need someone who is not afraid to tell us the truth, so choose someone who is not going to tell you what you want to hear, but what you need to hear.

In your search for a confidante, avoid developing a critical or judgmental spirit toward your wife. Without realizing it, you can criticize her for things that may be out of her control. Try not to analyze why she acts a certain way, which can consume you with what-if assumptions. Rebuke the spirit in the name of Jesus, and then seek Him for wisdom on how to handle the matter.

A common mistake is thinking that you are not supposed to be affected by relationship issues. You will be affected. You can be so concerned about what outsiders think that you pretend everything is fine. You can't share every situation with everyone because not everyone can handle your relationship issues. Embarrassment and pride can trick you into trying to resolve things alone. From time-to-time, you may question why you have relationship problems. As a pastor, I am not exempt for marital issues. I counsel couples and still have challenges with my wife. I must be the first partaker of the advice I share with others. God cares about what you care about. Let the Holy Spirit lead you. Pour out your heart to your wife, let her know what you are feeling, and then listen. Try to get to the root cause of the problem, which may require professional help. In any case, make yourself available. Ask God to help you not be offended by what your wife may say during counseling sessions. If you react in a negative way to what she says during a counseling session or a discussion at home, she may shut down and not share her true feelings anymore. When it comes to making improvements in your marital relationship, focus on being a better husband. You are the only person you can control. If you work on you and your wife works on herself, your marriage will blossom. Your goal is not to outdo the Joneses, but become a better version of you, individually and collectively.

Reflect

What makes it difficult to stick-and-stay in your marriage?

What helps you stick-and-stay in your marriage?

Have you ever asked God what His promise is for your marriage?

Do you have a confidante you can talk to about your marriage?

Love Note to Ladies

♥ When your husband does not respond to you the way you prefer, he may be walking in obedience to God, staying silent and letting the Lord handle the situation.

Chapter 12

God's Men Teach Their Children the Importance of Healthy Relationships

Children do not develop healthy relationships by osmosis. Before they are master mimics, it is essential that they see the dynamics—good and bad—of healthy relationships. And since parents are the first teachers, it's your job to teach by example. Your children watch how you interact with your spouse, parents, and people in general. If they see you being loving, caring, and kind, chances are they will do the same. The same is true if you are mean, belligerent, and selfish. Modeling good, productive behavior is not just for your wife. Take the lead to show your children healthy relationships filled with mutual love, respect, and compassion. The fruit of the Spirit listed in Galatians 5:22-23 are valuable character traits for any relationship dynamic and reciprocal expression of feelings without fear of retaliation is powerful.

Because love is an action word, they need to see your love in action. Let them see your tenderness and affection toward their mother. Show them how important they are to you with your undivided attention. Provide them with firsthand experience of morality, manners, and motivation.

To ensure your children learn conflict resolution, they need to observe tension. Too many parents argue in front of their children, and then go into another room to resolve it. In that environment, children are learning how to disagree, but not how to agree to disagree. When the severity of the conversation requires remedy away from the children, explain the process and outcome to them...together. If you want your children to be rational critical thinkers and problem solvers, show your process to them in age-appropriate ways.

Another way to instill healthy relationship values is acknowledging positive interaction with siblings and friends.

Help your children develop standards for friendships and relationships. Set the bar high for how your daughter should be treated. Teach your son the principles of manhood: protect and provide. Although you cannot choose whom your children will marry, you can be the benchmark for quality.

Because I am no longer married to the mother of my children, I am diligent about maintaining quality relationships with my ex-wife and my children.

During the separation, my former wife moved into a different home. The emotional health of my family was important, so I had individual conversations with all three of my children: Cayla, Maya, and Camen, who were 13, 19 and 21 years old, respectively. I needed to know their thoughts and feelings about the pending divorce. I explained that the decision to segment our family was not mine; however, I was not going to force their mother to stay. I told them that I wanted her to be happy and I was not going to stand in her way. I chose my words carefully so as not to infer blame or inadequacy on their mother. Disrespecting her would only serve to damage my children. Although I was no longer responsible for covering my ex-wife, I was responsible for being peaceful, respectful, and kind.

When I asked how they felt about the separation, they focused on me as a father. They expressed how I had been there for them and belief that I would continue to be there. They wanted both parents to be happy.

My son, Camen, said, "I have never seen you mistreat Mom. Just because what you tried didn't work in the marriage, doesn't mean that what you did was bad."

I explained that despite not being able to stay together as husband and wife, marriage is good. Thank God, my children were emotionally solid. I did not have to overcompensate trying to convince them of my love or compete with their mother for theirs.

Reflect

What does a healthy relationship look like to you?

What can you do to create a healthy relationship?

As a child, did anyone teach you — formally or informally — the importance of healthy relationships?

Love Note to Ladies

♥ Share with your husband your perspective of a healthy relationship.

A man who isolates himself seeks his own desire; he rages against all wise judgment.
A fool has no delight in understanding, but in expressing his own heart.
When the wicked comes, contempt comes also; and with dishonor comes reproach.
— Proverbs 18:1-3

Chapter 13

God's Men Leave a Legacy

A good man leaves an inheritance to his children's children, but the wealth of the sinner is stored up for the righteous.

—Proverbs 13:22

What do you want to leave your family? Be a vision caster to create and execute a plan for your family long after you're gone.

Memories

My father left me with great memories and life lessons about how to be the man of the family. He taught me the importance of providing for my family and being involved with every aspect of a child's life. His legacy included generating multiple streams of income and never feeling like I was above doing any job.

Spend quality time with your wife and children to create memorable moments. Attend school events, take family vacations, and worship together at home and church.

Money

What kind of financial planning are you doing to ensure your family maintains their lifestyle when you are dead? Will their inheritance be outlined in a legitimate will or will they have to "pass the hat" or launch a fundraising campaign to cover your funeral expenses?

I have extensive conversations with my children about money management including paying God first, paying yourself next, and then saving for retirement. I encourage them to put aside money for emergencies, pay bills on time, and have a fun fund.

Dave Ramsey is a Christian authority on wealth. He identifies *7 Baby Steps to Build Wealth*[16]] that pairs practical tools with biblical principles:

1. Save $1,000 for your starter emergency fund.
2. Pay off all debt, except your home, using the debt snowfall.
3. Save three to six months of expenses in a fully-funded emergency fund.
4. Invest 15% of your household income into retirement.
5. Save for your children's college funds.
6. Pay off your home early.
7. Build wealth and give.

Ministry

This legacy is far more valuable than your processions and your children don't have to wait until you die to receive it: the spiritual deposit of God. Sharing your identity in Christ with your children

---

[16] *Dave Ramsey's 7 Baby Steps to Build Wealth,* DaveRamsey.com online: https://www.daveramsey.com/dave-ramsey-7-baby-steps (accessed April 30, 2020).

will help them create positive memories, make sound decisions, and live with a godly moral compass. Your spiritual legacy will yield great harvests for generations.

Dr. Myles Monroe had profound insight into vision and legacy:

"Vision is the ability to see beyond what your eyes can see."

"When you believe in your dream and vision, it begins to attract its own resources. No one was born to be a failure."

"Don't die old, die empty. That's the goal of life. Go to the cemetery and disappoint the graveyard."

Be a vision caster with forward thinking; see the big picture, and then share it with your family. Even if they don't understand or agree with God's vision for you, your job is to see it to completion. Their approval is not a prerequisite for the vision to manifest.

For as he thinks in his heart, so is he.
— Proverbs 23:7a

Paraphrasing Apostle Paul in 1 Corinthians 3:6-9, one plants, one waters, God gives the increase. When you share the vision with your children, you plant seeds. You may or may not see the results of these seeds, but know that God will bring your vision — His vision — to pass. King David wanted to build a temple for the Lord; however, because of his sin with Bathsheba and perpetual bloodshed, God reserved that privilege for his son, Solomon. Instead of wallowing in disappointment, the king prepared his son and stored construction resources (1 Chronicles 22). Prepare like David, be diligent like Noah, and faithful like Job regarding God's promises to you. If God gave you the vision, He will give you everything needed to manifest it. Don't surrender your joy, vision, or power. Be open to receiving wisdom, knowledge, and understanding from those who have already done what you are trying to do. Share your progress with your family. As they see your diligence and persistence, they may grab hold to the vision and provide ideas of their own.

I saw my son, Camen, as a vision catcher when he came home from college. We talked until 3:00 AM. During our conversation, Camen expressed understanding of advice I shared with him years earlier.

He approached me about an issue with one of his high school football coaches. He felt that the coach was treating him unfairly.

I asked, "Did you pray for him?" I wanted him to understand that prayer is the answer to every situation. I expressed the need to walk in integrity and not let the coach see that his actions bothered him. I encouraged him to have a one-on-one conversation with the coach to clear the air.

Camen earned a football scholarship to my alma mater, Valdosta State University (VSU). People joked about him breaking my records; however, I told them that I wanted him to break records in the classroom.

When he left for VSU, I told Camen that he was an ambassador for Christ and the Marshall name. I had established a reputation of kindness and godliness at VSU and expected him to keep it that way. I'm pleased to say that Camen represented well. He prayed at the end of practice. His teammates asked if he used notes to pray. They requested that he lead all team prayers because it felt different from the coach's prayers.

On another occasion, one of Camen's friends questioned whether men wrote the Bible and if the stories were fiction. Camen told him that the Bible is real and written by men inspired by God. Camen called me on three-way for further discussion. His impressive interpretation and impartation are my legacy.

My oldest daughter, Maya, called me one Sunday to tell me about a college experience.

"Daddy, I'm stressed about these finals." She paused. "I wasn't able to get to church, but I put on Gospel music and spent time with God."

"Good for you. Ask Him to help you recall what you already studied."

"When *Something about the Name of Jesus* [as performed by The Rance Allen Group] came on I, could not stop crying. It gave me strength to tackle my final exams."

"God hears your worship no matter where you are. I am so proud of you for going to God for assurance. Thank you for sharing your experience with me."

Her personal relationship with God blessed me. The reassurance that she had a solid foundation, especially when I wasn't there to catch her, confirmed that God had her covered.

My youngest daughter, Cayla, is serious about saving money. On the way to church, I often stop to give food or money to a homeless guy who sits in a store parking lot. This particular Sunday, I gave him all the cash I had.

Cayla reached into her purse. "Here, Daddy. Give him two more dollars."

She got it! The legacy of giving had been passed to Cayla.

Every good parent wants their children to have more than what they had. In getting more, be sure they get more Christ. Children need to know Jesus as soon as possible because they are facing different and greater challenges. But the answer is the same: reading, knowing, and living the Word.

I am the product of legacy. I am proof that prayers work. My successes outweigh my failures and that's a direct result of godly values instilled by my parents. I wish my father could see what God is doing in my life. I tell my mother that I am grateful I was born to her. She is the pattern for which I model my prayer life. She is blessed to see how her legacy operates in her children and grandchildren.

My sister has always been my biggest cheerleader. She reinforces the things I teach my children and she is part of the legacy that I am leaving them.

Know that everything you need to be the man God ordained you to be is already inside you. All you have to do is tap into your destiny. You are not what society says. You are the priest of your home.

About Carlos K. Marshall

While society, media, and politics often portray men in a negative light, author and speaker, Carlos K. Marshall, seeks to debunk the myth that all men are the same. His love for God and people speaks volumes through his pastoral messages of hope, healing, and inspiration. Best known for his honesty and loyalty, Carlos is adamant about rebuilding men who feel misunderstood, misdiagnosed, and mishandled — ushering them into a life of wholeness and headship. In addition to improving the physical man, Carlos has an innate gift to tap into the emotional, spiritual, and mental aspects.

As an advocate for the homeless and those who battle with mental illness, Carlos has global ministerial plans including The Holy Land, Africa, and Mexico. Whether inspiring men of various backgrounds and income levels, or sharing the Word of God from the pulpit, his greatest fulfillment comes from rearing his children, building a strong family, and motivating others to do the same.

CarlosKMarshall.com

Every way of a man is right in his own
eyes, but the Lord weighs the hearts.
To do righteousness and justice is
more acceptable to the Lord than
sacrifice.
— Proverbs 21:2-3

About Queen V Publishing

The Doorway to YOUR Destiny!

*Go thou and publish abroad
the kingdom of God.*

—Luke 9:60 ESV

Committed to transforming manuscripts into polished works of art, **Queen V Publishing** is a company of standard and integrity. We offer an alternative that allows the message in YOU to do what it was sent to do for OTHERS.

QueenVPublishing.com

Carlos K. Marshall